THE
PEDELKEE
STEAMER
ZIGTOOTINBURG, PA

*AN S.W. SANCTIONED
PRODUCTION*

CREATED AND WRITTEN BY
CHRISTOPHER VAUGHAN
COVER ART BY LADONNA VAUGHAN

Written and published by Christopher Vaughan

Cover art by LaDonna Vaughan

Copyright 2016

First Edition

ISBN 978-0-9863101-5-7

Table of Contents

Our steamship, fur manned
Sailed the River for glory
Glorps are made happy

Introduction

Who knew the great American novel needed a blue tree climbing lobster? Welcome back to round two of *Snootchie Woogums Presents: the Pedelkee Steamer!* In this edition, the question is answered, "What's a Pedelkee?" I hope it meets your satisfaction. Most likely, it will probably meet a passel of your satisfactions.

All of the various assortments are back in this adventure, and we introduce many new ones. (Well, at least several. That is, if you count species, and not actual individuals. Pedelkees number in the multiple thousands. [Dare I say, millions?] When the film is made, each Pedelkee will be listed individually, but no aliases will be allowed. Fortunately, mysteriousness is not a common trait among Pedelkees.) You will meet Jaime and Josslyn Crumbgrinder, not necessarily related. Your own personal Carrie Rugrat will make her appearance. There are no additional yardapes (thank goodness!) but both shipdog and science mentor are present.

The quota of varmints was doubled for this adventure, but only if you count the two denizens as varmints. Radio Free Debi even wins a prize. Also, a woody cup-shaped grandchild is launched into space. Look for, and dodge it, if you must.

Our tale centers around the Pedelkee Steamer, a proud, prize-winning, steam-powered, sailing ship, captained by the landlocked seafarer, the Olde Salte of a Sailor, himself. We sail for sightseeing and scientific purposes. A coat or jacket may be unnecessary because there are a scudillion amount of Pedelkees. (Only, if you look in Zigtootinburg, PA.)

"Steam a Pedelkee, today!" is #5 as found in the LJCV Reference Library under the Snootchie Woogums' Code of Fair Play

S. W. Sanctioned, of course!

A RUGRAT'S RETURN

Shannon Bo-Bannon came running up the path. As she burst into the group of children, she caught her foot on Lizzy-puppy's coat. Down she went into the pile. Rugrats, crumbgrinders, and various assortments of varmints went flying into the air.

"Shannon, what are you doing?" cried Carrie Rugrat.

Lizzy calmly stated, "My coat, my beautiful coat! I just got it at the Rawalpindi Department Store. What will Mr. Cracker say when he sees what you have done." (That is calm for Lizzy.)

"Oh, Lizzy-puppy, I couldn't possibly have hurt your coat. Remember, Mr. Cracker made it scuff-resistant when you bought it." (If you have been keeping track since the Introduction, you will have noticed a record set for accidentally, using hyphenated words.)

By this time, Shannon, Carrie, and Lizzy had been joined by the other various assortments. Into the group, came Sarah Butterwug (an indispensable member of the assortment), Rachel Bug, Jaime, and Josslyn Crumbgrinder (not necessarily related), and of course, the effervescent Melissa Flower. "Shannon, you must know something?" they all asked.

"Pedelkees! Pedelkees! They have come back! They want us to join them on the steamship," she gasped.

What news! It had been several years since the last appearance of those small furry creatures. Actually, appearance sounds far too casual, especially, when you consider there are thousands of the critters. (or millions. Check the movie credits!) Perhaps a better word would be "lingering entrance". But whatever the case, it certainly was good news. For whenever the Pedelkees appear, they bring with them the Pedelkee Steamer.

It is a magnificent ship that can carry each, and every one of the Pedelkees. (Quite a chore, if you stop and think about it. Well, are you?) Her captain is the Olde Salte of a Sailor, whose homeport is Zigtootinburg, PA. At least, that is what the emblem states on the bow:

Pedelkee Steamers-Zigtootinburg, PA.

(Bows are notoriously trustworthy!)

Wherever that is, the various assortments believe it is quite a distance from their home in the Quad-city Triplex. They know quite well that they live in the lesser parts of Woogumdom, so it is probably anybody's guess, where one could find Zigtootinburg, PA.

As mentioned, the Captain is the Olde Salte of a Sailor. He is a land-locked seafarer sailing the beautiful banks of the Monongahela River, nigh onto more years that a Pedelkee can count. He is as crusty as a cob, but as the great S.W. would say. "There's gold in them there heart mines". His particular ore shines its brightest whenever the Pedelkees choose to dock. For when the Pedelkees depart the Steamer, he is willing to accept a new crew consisting of rugrats, crumbgrinders, and various assortment of varmints.

Jaime Crumbgrinder was the first to speak. "Now Shannon, please get your breath. Look at your hair. How far did you run? If you turn around, I'll comb it for you."

With that pause, Carrie Rugrat chimed in, "Pedelkees! Oh, Shannon, I've wanted my own personal Pedelkee for as long as I can remember." (Carrie has wanted her own personal everything for as long as she can remember.) "How do we get one?"

Lizzy-puppy explained, "First of all, Carrie, there is no such thing as ever having just one Pedelkee." (Surprisingly, no exaggeration.) "You know they never live in smaller groups than a pack..." (So far so good. Yet, thousands, [or possibly millions] is a very large pack.) Besides, Snootchie Woogums told me..." (You surely knew it was only a matter of time before the exaggeration began.) "Pedelkees are NEVER, EVER for sale!"

All, at the same time, "Lizzy-puppy, you've met Snootchie Woogums?"

"Well, maybe he didn't tell me personally, but you know she can't buy one. But if she can buy a Pedelkee, I want one, too!"

"Hey, is Mr. Sailor giving Pedelkees away?" Josslyn Crumbgrinder (not necessarily related to Jaime Crumbgrinder) jumped into the conversation with her own characteristic fashion. She grabbed Rachel Bug's bright, red hair and pulled on it to exchange places within the circle. Rachel gave the traditional, "Yipes!", and punched Josslyn on her arm.

Please, do not misunderstand, Josslyn is never mean. Within Woogumdom, meanness is never found, with the possible exceptions of the once and multitudinous, one-winged Black Plover, and the nefarious Winston Chipmunk. (Softly, heard in the background are the opening notes to Beethoven's 5th symphony.) Even their meanness is entirely unintentional, they are just accidentally mean. But Josslyn does possess more than her share of orneriness. Perhaps, mischievous is a more accurate description of Josslyn's character, somewhat to the right of impish. Whatever the case, Josslyn joined the increasingly larger list of various assortments who desired a Pedelkee.

Rachel Bug said, "With my Pedelkee, I will let him sleep with me in my bed, forever," She is one of Lizzy-puppy's two sisters. The other being Sarah Butterwug (an indispensable member of the assortment.) Rachel Bug is 100% tomboy, not really ever at home unless she has dirt smeared on her cheek and a shoe half filled with sand. (Precisely measured, quartered and diced.) Some would say that she is just a little extremely talkative to the older assortments.

On the other hand, Sarah Butterwug is quiet. (The silence can be quite deafening at times.) She is the youngest of the sisters, and one of the smallest of the various assortments.

She is indispensable for her willingness to listen. There are many of them, and they tend to compete for speaking time. When no one else will listen, there is always Sarah. Of them all, she appears to have resisted the urge to own a Pedelkee. That's because she was listening to the effervescent Melissa Flower,

Stay around Melissa for long, and you feel as if you are looking into a glass of freshly poured soda pop. (*Schnoke,* of course.) 'Effervescent' certainly describes her. "Sarah, we are all missing the point. Pedelkees aren't to own...Pedelkees are to love!" (Yeah, me too. I get it. Insert gag reflex here.) "You are too young to remember the last time they came. The Captain took us all for a cruise through beautiful Blichtenstein, Ohio, (home of beautiful toads), and wait till I tell you about our cabin bunks. They were magnificent mahogany frames, dressed to look like stained plywood."

It was several minutes of constant chatter before Shannon caught the missing point, (fortunately, not the one that Melissa was making), while they were all visiting, no one was sailing on the Pedelkee Steamer. "Hey, we are all a bunch of knunk-n-heads. We are missing the boat!" Suddenly, seven heads snapped to attention with all their eyes upon Shannon. Even Sarah managed to control her listening long enough to come to order.

"If you follow me, I will take you all to the Pedelkees." (Just faintly heard in the background, "O-o-oh! Finally, I get to have my own personal Pedelkee!)

With that last dreamy comment, the various assortments went heading toward the particular bank of the Monongahela where Shannon had caught sight of the Steamer.

Soon a problem developed. Poor Shannon. She tried her best, but she just could not keep the assortments organized. Sarah and Rachel, being the smallest, could not go very fast, and some of the others had no desire to stay with the group. That would be Carrie and Josslyn. They had to lead, it is in their nature. One of them would get in front, and then the other would race ahead. Of course, only Shannon knew where the whole group was going, which led to all kinds of confusion when a turn in the path was required because Carrie and Josslyn did not know where they were going, but turned anyway. Each time a turn came up, Shannon screamed at the top of her voice for the two varmints to come back. If they heard her, they would return, but if they were too far ahead, one of the others had to catch up to them, and bring them back while the rest waited. You would expect Carrie and Josslyn to automatically return when they saw one of the others calling, and trying to catch up to them. For the first couple of times, they did, but this quickly became a game. By the third turn, one was telling the other varmint to take off even faster, when they heard their names being called. Eventually, they would slow down, and let that particular assortment catch up, but for the rest of the group this got old fast. They traded places trying to catch them at every turn, but of course, the two smallest could not help. There were just too many turns, and too few assortments to keep up the game. By the final turn, the two varmints were too far ahead, and the remaining assortments were too tired to chase them any longer. Shannon called and called, but this only resulted in Carrie and Josslyn getting farther away. Shannon was frustrated, and the others were exhausted.

Jaime did her best to console Shannon. It took several minutes for them to decide that it was better to wait rather than to try to catch the two rascals. Hopefully, the varmints would realize no one was following, and come back. That seemed like a false hope. Even though they tried hoping, the duo just did not come back.

To their credit, they eventually did realize no one was following, but not until the thirteenth turn. (It is always the 13th turn.) By that time, they were either too far ahead of the others, or the others were too far behind. Regardless of the situation, Carrie and Josslyn were lost.

"Shannon, if we stay here, they won't find their way back," cried Jaime. "If we try to find them, they will run away further. What are we going to do?"

"I think we ought to string them up," Lizzy-puppy volunteered. (Her sister, Sarah, stared with amazement. It was such concise, easy-to- execute plan. Sarah appreciates firm, logical discipline, yet almost never expects it from Lizzy.) She continued, "Then we can put them on a stick and carry them."

Shannon asked, "Lizzy, who is going to carry them?" (Lizzy pointed at Jaime.) "How does that help us find them?"

"I know how to find them."

Sarah Butterwug <u>spoke</u> that statement. She shocked the group with her comment. Her sister, Rachel dropped the mud pie she was making, and broke out with an enormous laugh. Shannon's eyes registered their widest aperture possible. (Aperture is too a word!) The rest of the assortment stopped talking, and stared at Sarah.

These were Sarah's very first words. After listening patiently all these years, she finally decided to talk.

"My sister, she can talk!" shouted the great Liz.

Melissa Flower cut her short with the comment, "Well, Lizzy, of course she can talk. There is a big difference between not wanting to talk, and not being able to talk. She just never found it important to say anything. I am so proud of you, Sarah. If you can help us get the others back, I'll do whatever I can to help."

"Sarah, what <u>can</u> we do to find Carrie and Josslyn?" asked Shannon.

Carrie and Josslyn had done the worst possible thing to do when you are lost. Instead of staying put, and letting the others find them, they tried to find the others. They just got more lost, and kept getting farther and farther away from the assortment.

"Carrie, this isn't working," cried Josslyn. "We're getting lost. It's your fault!"

"How can you say it is my fault that we are lost? Remember, you were chasing me when we ran off. I remember, saying, 'Chase me!' and you did. So it's your fault! I can't be blamed for your irresponsible behavior."

"But I only chased you because you dared me to catch you. I think that the person doing the daring, should get most of the blame. I can't be blamed for being easily influenced. I don't know why I listen to you, Carrie. If we ever get back, I swear, I will help Lizzy-puppy do it to you whatever she comes up with."

"Josslyn don't say that. Lizzy can come up with the worst punishments."

"And it won't even be logical. So, then you better hope Shannon and Jaime calm her down. If they don't, we will really get it."

"Actually, Josslyn, maybe it would be worth it, just to get found. Do you think we will ever be able to go shopping again?"

"Carrie, there is more to life than shopping!" screamed Josslyn.

"Josslyn, how can you say that? Take that back! Why, just last week Melissa and I were...wait, Josslyn! Did you hear that? Coming from over there! We're saved! Help is coming from <u>that</u> direction." She pointed over in that direction.

With that cry, Carrie jumped, and started running like gangbusters. Josslyn started running right behind her, and yelling at her to explain, but Carrie would not be sidetracked. Off they ran until they broke out of the woods, and into a clearing. There in front of them were the others. As she reached the group, Carrie collapsed at Shannon's feet. With her last conscious breath, she uttered, "Where? Where? Where...where is the sale?"

The various assortments of rugrats, crumbgrinders, and varmints broke into laughter. Sarah's plan worked to perfection. It was her idea for all of the assortments to begin shouting **'Fashion sale! Fashion sale! Rawalpindi fashion sale!'** This was aimed into the general direction of Josslyn and Carrie. Sarah knew it would be only a matter of time before Carrie's shopping radar would zero in on their oral advertisement. (or if you prefer, advertisement) Within moments, Carrie heard the ad, and was hot on the sale's trail. It would take a few minutes for the two crumbgrinders to recover their breath before the assortment could resume their trip, but this time they would all travel together.

As Snootchie would say: "It's better to listen to a little weasel than to ignore an old toad any day."

A Steaming We Will Go

Truly, the Pedelkee Steamer, was a magnificent ship. Its twin stacks rose high into the sky. From bow to stern, it was built over 700 feet long. The paddleboat was a three-decker with a Pedelkee hanging out of every hole and window. (It's nearly impossible to do that with only a two-decker.) Rather than trailing behind the craft, the paddlewheels were built onto the outer-middle of the ship, one on each side. On its bow, stretching from starboard to port (but not vice versa) a sign clearly painted, so all could read:

PEDELKEE STEAMERS-ZIGTOOTINBURG, PA.

While you could not see the Captain, all the assortments could clearly hear him shouting his orders on deck to his Pedelkee shipmates: "Avast, ye swabs! Fistle them Blinkenknoggers! Thinkin' you're still amongst them Bowl-a-Far bosses. I knew that ole Boogums and Booter would be too easy on ye. I want this ole darlin' tub shipshape and ready for bear. Don't be thinkin' you can bribe me to be gettin' out of your work!"

That was always the Captain's signal that his bark was much worse than his bite. It was a prearranged moment. A given Pedelkee would come forward and offer the Olde Salte his favorite snack: candy orange slices. You see, the Pedelkees are actually the owners of the Steamer, and not its employees. Many, many years ago, they formed a partnership with the Olde Salte when he first became a landlocked seafarer, and asked him to sail between the banks of the Monongahela River. Pedelkees love sailing the beautiful Monongahela River more than anything else in the world. They just prefer to do their sailing in a steamship. They are also quite good at it. They have set several sailing records using the Pedelkee Steamer as their flagship.

None of the assortments was more glad to arrive than Melissa. She had used up every bit of her abundant effervescence to satisfy Rachel's questions:

"Are we there yet?"

"Melissa, look at this bug?"

"Are we there yet?"

"How many steps have we taken?"

"Are we there yet?"

"If we were going to China, are we going in the right direction?"

"Are we there yet?"

Needless to say, after answering Rachel's questions for the thousandth time, Melissa was eager to arrive at the Pedelkee Steamer. The Pedelkee Steamer was looking forward to hosting them, but the ship could never be fully prepared for what was to come.

As all the various assortments broke through the woods, the first thing they saw was the sign. Eight youthful voices all broke out at once: "PEDELKEE STEAMER! We're here, Shannon, we've made it!" (For some reason, even Shannon was yelling the last part. There are times that the assortments all tend to think as one, and all yell, or say the exact same thing.)

The second thing they saw were the Pedelkees. Hundreds of them! Thousands of them! Dare we say, (in true Lizzy-puppy fashion) millions of them! (This sounds familiar.) There were so many of them that at a distance, one could not distinguish individuals. They appeared almost as a solid mass: oozing, vibrating, and weaving back and forth.

Pedelkees are similar to Pikas, having no tail, but are somewhat smaller. Pedelkees also like to sail, and I am not aware of a similar trait among Pikas. However, it must be said in all fairness, Pikas make a much better haystack than any number of Pedelkees. Neatness and precision counts.

Carrie and Josslyn, in characteristic fashion, ran the fastest, and first to reach the pack of Pedelkees, or herd if you prefer. (Pedelkees prefer the term 'passel'.) When Carrie saw the Pedelkees, she began squealing, "My own personal Pedelkee!" (Uncharacteristically, Josslyn said nothing.) Just before the two girls reached the pack, (technically: passel) the Pedelkees saw them approach, (more accurately: heard Carrie), and began their own high-pitched squeal. (Low volume, of course. The Olde Salte hates loud noises unless they are his own.) Immediately, the Pedelkees recognized Carrie and Josslyn, and were excited to have the two rugrats plunge into the pack (or passel.)

What a sight! It was as if they were swallowed whole by the Pedelkees. They both simply disappeared into the Pedelkees. Seeing that happen, the rest of the assortment stopped in their tracks. With her mouth, wide open, and not understanding the game, Sarah grew terrified. She began to edge herself, backwards. No longer did Pedelkees seem playful or harmless. Instead, Pedelkees appeared to be a community organism that ate little girls.

After a few seconds, or an eternity to the youngest one, Carrie and Josslyn emerged like they were spit out of a geyser. They were thrown fifteen feet into the air, but the thousands (Lizzie remembered, millions) of Pedelkees gently cushioned the duo's fall. Then it was repeated all over again. The older assortments began to laugh because of the antics of the Pedelkees. However, Sarah and her sister, Rachel were not laughing. The two smallest varmints had been too young to go on the last voyage of the Pedelkee Steamer, and knew nothing of what to expect from Pedelkees. Being concerned for the girls, Sarah pulled on Melissa's pocket and asked, "Should we rescue them?"

Melissa answered, "No. Join them." And they did.

Shannon grabbed Jaime's hand, Jaime took Rachel's hand, and Rachel took Sarah's hand, Melissa took Sarah's other hand, while Lizzy-puppy completed the chain by taking Melissa's hand. They charged into the pack (or passel) to join Carrie and Josslyn and promptly disappeared into the Pedelkees.

Somewhere, deep into the passel, (finally, someone got that right!) one could barely hear, "My own personal Pedelkee. I will take this one...no, that one. No, maybe you!"

As Snootchie would say, "Why sugarcoat trampolines, when you can have Pedelkees bake bread right from the grocery." So that explains why by this time, the Olde Salte fistled his last blinkenknogger, and put a stop to Operation Geyser. He swaggered down the gangplank. (The Captain has magnificent sea legs. They even won a prize.) He called everyone to order.

Before they could assemble, Melissa Flower whispered to Rachel Bug, "He is wearing his navy-blue sailing coat with white cap, and white leggings. Last time, he chose his optional puce peg leg with red legging. I liked that uniform, but in this one, he looks quite dashing."

Indeed, he did. Besides the prize for his sea legs, the Olde Salte was named, *Sartorial Sailor,* three years in a row. (Yet never consecutively.) Bear in mind, that it is his aesthetic choice to wear the captain's peg leg. Perhaps, it gave Heidi the idea for her eye patch. (It only gave him severe leg cramps.)

At last, getting everyone at attention, he called for the oldest assortment, "Commodore Shannon Bo-Bannon, present your crew!" She introduced some and re-introduced most. He assigned titles and work details.

"I am the Chief Prettiest officer," announced Jaime.

"You are!" answered Shannon, "But really you are the Chief Petty Officer."

"I am Chief Executive Officer Melissa."

"I am Lieutenant Lizzy, master and commander! Lord of all I purvey! Purvey me and tremble!" (Lizzy even had brought an admiral's bicorn hat!)

"I am General Nuisance Carrie."

"I am Major Headache Josslyn."

"I am Midshipman Plus Rachel."

"I am Position to be named later, Sarah."

The Olde Salte had his crew with one exception. "Arrrgh! We've no one to man the poop-deck."

Sarah took one look at Rachel and said, "That is a job for yardapes, if I have ever heard one!"

Who should arrive, as if on cue, and courtesy of the Over-Priced Goat Taxi, (please, NO loud noises!) but Blackjack Jason, the ice pirate, Sir Harold, the sheriff of Woogumdom County, their shipdog, Heidi, the pertack Docksoon, and Squirrely Jo Peterson, our vacationing teacher, mentor and our science conference speaker, and dachshund extraordinaire! (Optional traditional monocle, mandatory.)

Jason spoke up after the taxi pulled away very quietly. "It gives us great pleasure that we have come to say 'bone vay-odgeey' to our girls in every port, Rachel Bug and Sarah Butterwug. One of us is looking forward to the traditional goodbye kiss!" This left out Sir Harold, since both were his sisters.

"We'd be honored to give a goodbye kiss…to HEIDI!" shouted Sarah. "And it's pronounced *bon voyage*." That did not seem to make any difference to the yardapes. They make up too many words, to keep track of real ones.

Hearing Sarah's voice for the first time, Jason took full credit. "My Butterwugness! Just the hope of getting a Blackjack kiss, and you breaks out with a voice of joy. I is a miracle worker."

"You is delusional!" she yelled. "I mean are."

18

Pushing Sarah out of the way, Rachel added, "If we kiss you, we could break out in a rash!"

Harold punched Jason in the arm and told him, "They are fighting to be first in line. Jason, you are girl magic! However, I am holding out for a kiss from Shannon Bo-Bannon. Are you sure she likes younger guys?"

Being Shannon's brother, Jason answered, "Harold, you might already be too old for her." On that, Shannon was rescued from a fate worse than death.

By this time, the dachshunds were giving rides to innumerable Pedelkees. Heidi kept Pedelkee size saddles under her eye patch for just such occasions. She remembered not to bring Pedelkee sized whips. Experience is the best teacher. In her honor, some Pedelkees were seen wearing eye patches, while others wore the traditional monocle. One wore a monocle and an eye patch. (It was a German Pedelkee.)

Having assembled a full crew and believing that he was out of range of the twenty Blue Dahlia Fainting Goats, the Olde Salte of a Sailor fired off the cannon salute. Much to the regret of Over-Priced, three fainting goats were not out of range from the cannon's sound blast. Waiting for the fainters to recover, made him late getting to his barber shoppe quartet concert.

The Captain, fully unaware of the fainting, winked at Commodore Shannon, and she proceeded to order, "All aboard! Pull the gangplank, and full steam ahead!" Off they sailed to their destination.

Truth be told, the main function of the various assortments of rugrats, varmints, crumbgrinders, and yardapes was sightseeing.

Pedelkees did all the work, even on the poop deck, which disappointed the yardapes, especially finding out the true nature of a poop deck.

There was the mandatory lecture on 'the Migratory Patterns of Red and Green Tree Climbing Lobsters' as given by Ms. Peterson. The Captain sat through all three sessions, asking technical questions concerning arboreal crustaceans. Having won her respect, Ms. Peterson presented the Captain with the familiar Blue Tree Climbing Lobster, kept for such occasions, but not kept under Heidi's eye patch. Photos of the presentation were broadcast by Radio Free Debi on LJCV American Toad Radio.

The next morning, all were on deck, as the Pedelkee Steamer sailed up the beautiful Monongahela River. Both dachshunds were sunbathing on top of the poop deck. This was a result of a wager between them and the yardapes. Both pirate and sheriff were working in the galley doing the puppies' chores of cleaning the dishes. While sunbathing, the shipdog, and science conference speaker wore complementary sunglasses, azure blue.

It was Jaime Crumbgrinder that pulled on the Captain's white legging to ask a question. Bending down, the Captain asked, "Avast, ye Chief Prettiest Officer. What service may I do for you?" (Apparently, it does mean that!)

She curtsied and asked, "Captain, our heading? Blichtenstein, Ohio? (Home of beautiful toads.) Tegucigalpa, Mehico? Maybe some place new?"

"Well, CPO Jaime, I'm glad ye asked me. In nautical terms, we be a sailing up to the source of the beautiful Monongahela River, and dining at Lara's Place in Café Bowl-A-Far."

He continued, "Also, tell Ms. Peterson, when she be finishing her sun bath, that we be investigating the natural habitat of Rocky Mountain Oysters at the summit of ValleyTop Mountain. One of Squirrely Jo's ears shot straight up with anticipation. The tip of Heidi's tail wagged. (Excessively.) The assortments all gasped, and the Pedelkees made one collective smile.

To air is human, but two dachshunds are divine!

To What Part of this Man's Nasal,

Do you Belong?

ValleyTop is the highest peak in all of Woogumdom. Rising to 539 feet above the local Rawalpindi Department Store, one can see almost all of Woogumania, unless you are visiting the valley in the top of the summit. If you were there, you would be at Lara's Place in Café Bowl-A-Far, and then you'd be only at elevation 467 feet. Very difficult to see much from there unless you enjoy seeing the valley rise to the summit. (Even if it is just a valley rising up to a summit, the view is superb!)

Having set their destination, the Captain ordered, "Weigh anchor, or I'll give you Pedelkees a taste of the Commodore's daughter. (It really is a cat with nine tails!) Full speed, ahead." The Pedelkees pushed the throttle, and off they went, steaming upriver.

As they rounded the next turn, they encountered Radio Free Debi filming her next radio broadcast. She was in a speedboat with the Masked Toad and the Weasel of Wonder skiing behind her. In her boat, were their respective sidekicks: trusty Ace Burundi, and nonchalant Oon Sallemon, sitting nonchalantly. Debi pulled up to the Steamer. Fortunately, out of view of the various assortments, no one saw the Weasel of Wonder helping the Masked Toad stay above water, He is not very buoyant, having very few frog genes for a toad. At least, this is the explanation given by Professor Peterson, who should know, being an expert on arboreal crustaceans.

Radio Free Debi wanted volunteers for her current skiing adventure. A white one-winged Plover will carry the contestant, and place him/her on the shoulders of either toad or weasel while skiing. Graciously, the Weasel of Wonder allowed the Masked Toad to go first. Most of the Pedelkees volunteered, but so did Sir Harold, and Melissa Flower. Harold had Shannon hold his badge. He hoped it was the beginning of a wonderful relationship.

The Weasel got into the boat, and Debi took off pulling the Toad. Everyone was on the edge of their seat full of anticipation until they realized that no one had hired a white one-winged Plover. Everything came to a stop, while arrangements were made, and the Weasel came to the Toad's rescue. The Plover demanded extra wages for income lost due to the interruption of his friendly, pinochle game. Debi agreed to pay, even though she knew a Plover would never leave a pinochle game if he was winning. With the plover problem solved, Debi's boat was ready to take off.

Everything seemed to go according to plan. The Toad, while a horrible swimmer, was a tremendous skier. They assumed his feet made perfect skis. Debi maintained full speed as the Plover used his feet to swoop up Harold, and gently place him on the Toad's shoulders. No one had told the Toad to remove the suntan lotion from off of his shoulders. Harold made a perfect landing. However, Harold's feet slid off the Toad's shoulders just after the Plover released him. Up into the air, Harold flew until he decided that it was time to come down. His butt smacked the Toad on the back of his neck. The Toad fell into the river, and the boy held on to the Toad's superhero mask for dear life. Harold clung on top, and most of the Toad floated under water. It turns out that the Toad is a marvelous, underwater swimmer, and can hold his breath somewhat accurately. He managed to take Harold over to the Steamer, while Debi spun around, and picked up the Toad. Needless to say, the Toad was through for the day. As Harold climbed aboard deck, Shannon, in official capacity as commodore, pinned his badge back on, and kissed him on the cheek in military fashion. Harold collapsed onto the deck in a giggling heap in true yardape fashion. (He promised to never again wash that cheek, but that's not much of a promise for a yardape!) For this skiing adventure to be successful, it would be up to the Weasel of Wonder, and Melissa Flower.

Checking first for Weasel suntan lotion, Melissa got ready for the Plover's liftoff. All passengers, and most of the crew were topside watching. Everything seemed in order. Everyone focused on ski boat in water. The boat took off with the Weasel in tow. The Plover took off with Melissa in feet.

Debi gave throttle, the bird gave chase, and the Weasel tensed with fear and trepidation. Plovers are widely known for their pinochle skills, but what few people know is their dedication to ballet. As he approached the Weasel, he spun performing a perfect pirouette. Melissa following his lead, and executed the standard triple Lutz, closing with a Bielman spin on the Weasel's head. Not to be outdone, the Weasel of Wonder, while shifting to a surfboard, jumped, catching Melissa in his arms, and hung eight, as he surfed toward the ship! (Among surfing weasels, it's common knowledge to judges that they never count the smaller inner toe as they cowabunga.)

Pedelkee judges gave the white one-winged Plover, a score of "98". (Pedelkees are tough ballet judges when scoring a perfect pirouette!) Then gave a perfect gymnastic "6" to Melissa Flower. (Extra points awarded for belly rubs that Melissa provided before the event. Pedelkees cannot be bought, but may be rented cheap!) The Weasel received an outstanding, surfing "10". Radio Free Debi was surprised by the judges with a presentation of 1st Place in racing competition! LJCV American Toad Radio set rating records when the film was broadcast in its entirety over the radio. Debi's fashion sense especially broadcasts well over the radio.

After the event, with full sails unfurled, Shannon gave the order, "Full steam ahead." Nothing happened! None of the steam engines, unfurled their steam. She looked at the Captain, and he shrugged his shoulders. He ran toward the pilot seat, and found Josslyn holding wrenches, and Carrie clutching the separated steamboat throttle.

He screamed, "Arrrgh! You scurvy, bilge, rugratted, crumbgrinders!" Carrie's meek defense, "I've always wanted my own personal steamboat throttle?"

The rest of the voyage was fairly uneventful. The Olde Salte regaled the shipmates with his tales of being a landlocked seafarer. One of his favorites: "Ahoy, mates! That's exactly how to put two quarts of jelly in a one quart jar, nautically speaking, of course." Closely followed with, "Arrrgh! If ye failed to fistle them blinkenknoggers the first time, why wouldn't ye fistle them again?" Finally, his best story, "Identify one Pedelkee? That's easy. That one!" Nobody tells a story like the Olde Salte.

As the story-telling progressed, Sarah, Rachel, Jason, and Harold snuck into the Captain's quarters to see the familiar Blue Tree Climbing Lobster. Neither dachshund was with them. Both dackels were sharing quaffs of root beer with their fellow Pedelkees. Not all dogs enjoy root beer, but it is a particular favorite among dachshunds and beagles.

Sarah pulled on Rachel's shoulder, "Should we even be here?"

Before she could answer, Jason spoke. "Didn't the Captain tell us to explore the ship? Isn't this part of the ship? Besides, what could go wrong?"

It was a tossup who looked at who first, even Harold stared at Jason. So Jason said, "WHAT? WHAT DID I SAY?" Rachel put her finger up to Jason's mouth, and told him to hush. "Now, my Bugaciousness, don't get all romantical on me. This is not a double-date."

Sarah held her gag reflex, and Harold did not. He refused to double date his sisters. "Can we just get on with it, before we get caught in here."

27

All four walked over to window, and expected to see the lobster in the terrarium by the porthole, but it was not there. Next to the window was the Captain's palm tree that he won in his first sailing race. Sarah suggested that perhaps the lobster climbed the tree.

Jason pushed her out of the way, and stared up into the palms. "I can't see a thing. Harold, bring that lantern over here." He did. "Okay, that's better. By the way, how will I know, if I'm finding the right one? What color is this blue lobster, anyway?"

"BLUE!!!" They shouted.

"Oh!!!" He scratched his head. "I think I see it, way up there. Hoist me up, ladies. Harold, give me the lantern! Girls, hold me. Hah! You both are holding your man...Ouch!!!!" He yelled, as they dropped him to the floor, but Harold caught the lantern.

Promising to keep his remarks to himself, they lifted Jason and his lantern back up into the palm tree. "Okay, he's right above me. I'll blind him with the lantern, and grab him, and then we'll..." Jason never finished his sentence. The Blue Tree Climbing Lobster reacted in his familiar pattern when blinded. It was a bid for survival practiced in the deepest oceans of Delta Junction, Alaska. While holding onto a palm branch with one claw, it swung down, and squeezed Jason by his nose with its other. In Ms. Peterson's lectures, she noted that blues have the strongest pinching power of any of the climbers.

Jason screamed, "Get it off! GET IT OFF! HURRY! THAT'S THE NOSE I BREATHE WITH! OW! IT HURTS!! IT HURTS!!!"

They dropped Jason, and still the critter hung on. The palm tree bent down to Jason's level. Harold and Rachel grabbed Jay, and Sarah pulled on the lobster. It was a tug of war that Jason would have been proud to watch, but to no avail. Jason was caught *in nasal de lecto.*

Sarah came up with an idea, "Harold! Open the window! We'll throw the palm out the window, and that will make the lobster let go." Rachel agreed to go along with the plan.

Harold argued, "We can't throw the tree into the river."

Sarah answered, "Hello! There's a **deck** outside the window. After Jason gets loose, we'll bring the palm back in, and put the lobster in the terrarium."

"Can we hurry! My nose is gonna fall off." Harold opened the window, and the girls heaved the palm tree.

To a certain extent, the plan worked. The lobster let go of the palm tree, but still hung onto Jason's nose. "Now, what do we do?"

It was then that the door flew open, and in walked the Olde Salte of a Sailor and his commodore, Shannon Bo-Bannon. She was carrying Squirrely Jo. The Captain held Heidi, the shipdog. She jumped from his arms, and proved why she is an attack dachshund. She charged, and promptly pulled Jason's pant leg, tripping him onto the floor. It absolutely did no good, and served no useful purpose, but she did maintain her reputation.

Using her paws, Squirrel pulled a bottle of root beer from her attaché case, and applied one drop to the lobster's nose, or its approximate location. It is not well known, but lobsters cannot hold their root beer.

29

Feeling the world spinning, the crustacean let go of Jason's nose, and fell to the ground, but not before losing its entire supper of old locust skins, and vomited them right onto Jason's face. This did not taste like chicken!

The Captain picked up the tipsy lobster, and it slept off its stupor in the terrarium. The Olde Salte asked, "Where is me prize palm tree?"

Rachel stammered, "On the deck outside your window?"

"Arrrgh, matey! There be no deck outside me window."

All turned and glared at Sarah. Even the lobster hiccupped in her direction. She stammered, "Hopefully, the Captain intends that figuratively."

"No, darlin', me intent is literally no deck."

"Oh! This night can't get any worse," she said sadly.

Jason, holding back tears through his vomit covered face, answered, "I think it just did! Something tells me that I am allergic to shellfish!"

The Journey of 600 Yards Starts with a Tent? Bears and Acorns are Included!

The yardapes and the smallest assortments discovered the meaning of KP. It does not mean: *Kool Privileges*. Apparently, the yardapes displayed real expertise in swabbing decks, figurative or otherwise. The girls: not so much. However, showing true growth in character, the Blue Tree Climbing Lobster swore off root beer except for special occasions.

The wind turned as they headed toward ValleyTop Mountain, and with it, just the slightest hint of revenge, a dish best served cold.

The Steamer landed at the docks at the foot of ValleyTop. Crew and passengers disembarked from the vessel. Pedelkees, and most of the assortments hiked up the trail, taking the fork to the left. Shannon, Jaime, the Olde Salte, and the great Liz took the spoon to the right. Following this small expedition were the two dachshunds. Heidi was wearing a blue bandanna with yellow polka dots, and the reliable eye patch. Squirrel wore her Teutonic silver, scientific, hiking britches, carrying the aforesaid attaché case, and wearing her mobile eyepiece.

Lizzy took command of the situation. "Alright, Jaime. Command check for Survival kit. Twelve person tent?"

"Check," said Jaime.

Shannon interrupted, "Lizzy, why do we need a 12 person tent?"

"Emergency housing for survivors, my Commodore," answered Liz.

"But, Lizzy, we are only 600 yards from the summit. If we go very far, we could come back to the ship, or go on up to Lara's Place," pleaded Shannon.

"That's why they call them disasters, Sir!" The great Liz saluted smartly. "Why an earthquake could hit. A blizzard could strand us for days. An accidental medical emergency could happen, and here we have a temporary hospital right here at the base of the mountain. A typhoon, cyclone, tsunami, hurricane, tornado, whirlwind, or a nor'easter could blow in. Famine, draught, pestilence, or prickly itch could devastate our little community. Well, not on my watch, Sir!" Liz adjusted her bicorn hat. "I am Lieutenant Lizzy, master and commander, standing in the gap, guarding the gates!"

Shannon interrupted. "Liz…" Lizzy shot her a look. "I mean Lieutenant Lizzy. Who's going to carry all of these supplies? There's only the four of us?"

Lizzy answered, "Why, Jaime of course. That's the whole point of having a CPO. Lieutenants get to give them orders."

Jaime dropped her jaw as she looked at Liz. "Why me?" she asked.

"Well, the dachshunds are pretty much loaded up, already. Besides, Squirrely Jo is our scientific mentor and all." Heidi flashed Liz that look. Lizzy immediately recognized that look. "Heidi would flat out refuse any of my orders."

(If shipdogs could 'harrumph', Heidi just gave one.) Turning her attention back to the others, Lizzy continued, "Shannon and the Captain are fellow officers," (under her breath she said, "Almost my equals!"), "and that only leaves CPO Jaime, as the trusted enlisted person to carry out all my orders."

Jaime blew up! "I am not a cart wagon for your personal whims and orders. It took me several hours just to take this stuff from the ship."

The great Liz responded immediately. "Insubordination! Insubordination!! Court-martial!!! I demand an immediate keelhauling! Where's our brig? Who is our Security Officer? Do we brand in this here navy?"

The Captain had heard enough. "Lieutenant Lizzy, Your title is only active aboard me boat. And seein' that we be on land, I am thinking that Chief Prettiest Officer Jaime is within her duties to just stroll with us up this here mountain, and not be used as a pack horse. As for this disaster drill, I be thinking' that could be put off to a later voyage. You would be welcome to join us, or perhaps you would like to stay behind, and be putting this all back?"

"Well, I g-g-guess that this could be put off till later. We are p-p-pretty shipshape, already," stammered Lizzy. The Captain nodded his head. Looking down and under her breath, she said, "I guess that I could drop all charges."

Jaime and Heidi stifled, "Harrumph!" Heidi never missed an opportunity to chide the great Liz, especially after the four-wheel drive buggy incident. (Which of course, resulted in the tip of her tail being broken.) Jaime and Heidi have one other joy in unity versus the Great Liz: they both enjoyed knowing that Lizzy's bicorn hat was on backwards.

It was around the bend that they first heard the wild denizens of ValleyTop. Carefully climbing up a large boulder, and keeping completely out of sight, the four of them peered over the top. The dachshunds were held by Shannon and CPO Jaime.

Coming down the path that crossed a stream running into the Monongahela River, they saw a large, brown bear with a big tan tummy. He had a nearly, bald face and was wearing glasses. It was Steve the Bear. He was singing.

♫ "I'm cruisin', I'm smoozin'! ♪ I'm lookin' for some food! ♪ I'm lookin' for acorns, today! ♪ My tummy is growlin'! My smile is a frownin'! ♪ My hunger has a mood! ♪ Let's go get some acorns, today!" ♫

Steve was happy because he knew that Bryan the Oak had the best acorns. Bryan was an old oak tree that unfortunately, Steve visited often. Bryan's face was easily seen in his bark. He had a prominent reddish, blonde mustache and a forehead that pushed thru the bark on his bough. He had just the slight hint of spectacles. He had many branches filled with acorns.

Bryan was no more than a few feet from Steve, when Steve changed his tune. Seeing Bryan took his mind off of eating.

♫ "Let's rub and dub! ♪ Instead of eatin' acorns. ♪ My bottom need a rubbin' on that tree! ♪ I'll glide and slide my bottom up and down! ♪ I'm rubbin' on that tree, all day!" ♫

Bryan could see where this was heading. "Don't put that big butt of yours over here. I am not some bark encased backscratcher. Go on, get away! You will find my bark is worse than your bite, you overgrown throw-rug!"

Ignoring Bryan, Steve sauntered over to Bryan, and rubbed his shoulder on him as if Steve was some giant cat. Bryan tolerated this, but Steve moved past his shoulder, and began to rub his hip on Bryan. If Bryan could draw a line in the sand, or a notch on his bark, this would be it.

"That's far enough, you itchy, scratchy, flea bag." Yet, it was not far enough for Steve. He turned his massive body around and began to back up into Bryan.

All Bryan could see was this massive butt pointed at his face. "Man, I wish I was a **PIN** oak, right now! I'd teach you to use me as a massage implement. Back away, you tan-tummied ursine, or I swear you will wish you had." Steve ignored him. "Alright, I warned you, and now you will get it!"

Steve just smiled. He again, ignored Bryan and began to sing.

♫ "Rubbin' on the ole oak tree! ♪ Just my true love, my hiney and thee! ♫ I will see you in September with an orange I'll remember, ♪ at the ole oak tree!" ♫ The song ended suddenly, "EEE-OUGH-WOO! WOO! That smarts!!!"

Bryan kept his word. Rather than using an acorn, (after all, they are his offspring,) Bryan shoved a hard-oak splinter right into Steve's gluteus, muchimous maximus. Steve began screaming, "Get it out! Get it out!"

Bryan would have none of it. "I have relinquished ownership. It is your splinter now. Based on where it's at, I am not touching it. You are on your own."

Before Steve could answer, a white one-winged Plover suddenly arrived. Plovers are Woogumdom's Messenger Service, somewhat unreliable. Landing squarely in the middle of them both, the Plover addressed Bryan.

"Either of yew gents, happen ter be Mister Bryan de Oak, Esquire?"

Steve would not let him answer, "White birdie, I gots a splinter in my booty! Can you help a poor, defenseless ursine?"

"Dat depends, bub. I see what is innit for yew, but what is innit fer me? How ken yew entice me to beak yer bottom, and remove said splinter?"

Knowing his opponent, Steve said the magic word. "Me and my buddies are pinochle-playin' fools." Halfway through this sentence, the Plover had already removed said splinter, and was spitting it out by the exclamation point.

Bryan brought the attention back to him. "What about Bryan the Oak?"

While removing a bit of fur from his beak, the Plover asked, "Are yew the aforementioned, de Oak?"

"Yes, I am," replied Bryan.

"Ken yew prove that yew reside at this residence?" asked the Plover.

"I am a blasted tree, you bird brain! I'm rooted here!" shouted Bryan.

"Whoa, bub. As a certified agent of Woogumdom's Messenger Service with the proper decals, I deliver only to proper gents. This here note cannot go to just any oak."

Bryan gave him the only evidence that the plover would accept. "Then on the official rulebook of pinochle, I swear that I am Bryan the Oak."

The Plover wiped a tear from his eye, as he accepted the oath. "I has a special delivery letter for yew from yer Mutter. She wants yew to visit her."

"You have read my letter?" Bryan asked.

"Only fer securitorial reasons, friend Oak."

"And how does she expect me to visit her?" Bryan was puzzled.

"That's easy," said Plover, "she says, make like a tree and leaf."

Steve started guffawing, and rolling on the ground. "Hee! Hee! Harumphthee Hee! Bryan, you must be cross-pollinated. That kinda sappy joke could only come from a sugar maple!"

Bryan grabbed an acorn, and threw it up Steve's enormous nose.

"Now, why'dja do that? You threwed it up me nosethb! Ah can't breethed! Help me pull it outhed. If you don't helph me, ah'll haff to blast it out!"

"What do you mean, *blast it out*? You ain't got no dynamite." Then it hit Bryan…figuratively. "Turn around! Turn around!! Point it away from me!"

Bryan shoved Steve with all of his might, and accidentally pointed the projectile at the four voyagers from the Pedelkee Steamer. The Olde Salte pulled Lizzy and Jaime with Squirrel down to safety. and Heidi, ever vigilant, jumped, and pulled Shannon down in the nick of time.

Steve took a deep breath, sneezed,   and grunted, "Thar she blows!"

Kaboom!!!

All four sailors felt the heat, and heard the acorn whiz by overhead. Steve shouted, "I have got an acorn in orbit!"

"Hey," said the Plover. "That gives me an ideer. If yew ken't visit yer Mum, let her see some grandkids." The Oak tree problem was solved. The Plover would take a bunch of acorns to see their grandmum with a note from Bryan.

The Plover had one more bit of business. "Whose comin' to de pinochle?"

Rubbing his nose, Steve said, "My best buds, the Rocky Mountain Oysters."

Heidi went into full alert. She began pulling Shannon up the path. Not wanting to hear more, the Captain snuck his other charges away from the denizens, over the creek, and up the path. They had no time to lose.

Lara's Place

The two dachshunds raced ahead of their partners. (Dachshunds frown on the use of the word, <u>owner</u>.) It was all the others could do to keep up with them.

"Shannon, why are <u>we</u> running? Why are the <u>dogs</u> running?" Jaime hollered.

Trying to keep pace with Jaime, Shannon answered, "Only they know. I was trying to keep pace with them!"

Hearing that, both dogs came to a stop over a hundred yards from where they left Bryan and Steve. As the others caught up, Heidi released Squirrel's attaché case, and the **'noted'** dachshund nuzzled in, and flipped a card to Lizzy.

The card read: **No time to lose!**

Jaime countered, "What's the hurry?"

Squirrel flipped another card to Lizzy: **Rocky Mountain Oysters must be observed under normal conditions of natural habitat per scientific regulation #354.b.**

All three of the various assortments uttered, "Oh!"

Then, one more card: **Pinochle is not recognized as 'normal', as per regulation #27.2578 addendum 4.**

The Olde Salte responded to all this card flipping, "We been awondering what it meant to be a **'noted'** dachshund. I think that she just showed us."

Then, the great Liz joined in. "If the Captain is the only one who knows where we can find the oysters' natural habitat, why are <u>they</u> leading? 'They' meaning the doggies, Shouldn't they be behind the Captain? At least, definitely behind the stalwart Lieutenant, master and commander of all that she purveys? Dachshunds have no military decorum. And I quote from, **Articles of Lizzie 221-15**." She turned to the dachshunds, and said, "Hah! to the doggies!"

In a flash, Shannon picked up Squirrel before she could retrieve one more card. No one wanted to know what that card said to Lizzie.

With equally quick thinking, the Captain motioned them off the path and into the woods. "Arrrgh! We can't find the Rocky Mountain Oyster by its lonesome. You have to find the host rock that be covering them. We be lookin' for a rock known as the Glorp."

Neither assortments, nor dogs had heard of a Glorp.

"Aye! Tis a sad tale of the Glorp. Originally, they were the predominant rock face in all of Woogumdom, but today, only a few representatives remain. 'Twas a relationship gone bad, I heard. The ones that be left, provide a sure refuge for the Rocky Mountain Oyster."

Jaime asked, "How will we know one?"

"That part be easy. Look for a large, sad-looking, purple rock that looks like half an egg buried into the ground. That be the Glorp."

Both Shannon and Jaime spoke, "That sounds so sad."

"Aye, that it is," agreed the Olde Salte.

"Let's split up from here, and go 100 feet, and look for the Glorp. Lizzy, go north. Jaime and Squirrel, go west. Shannon and Heidi, go south, and I be takin' east. Holler, if ye find anything. Go only in a straight line, and come right back here, if-n ye find nothin'. Proceed!"

Off they went, and very shortly all came back except Lizzy. The Captain gathered them, and headed north. Exactly 100 feet away was Lizzy, sitting on a rock, crying, and sucking on a peppermint stick. In between tears, she was moaning, "It's hopeless! Doomed to failure! Master and Commander, the Purveyor's Lost Expedition! Swallowed up into history's mysteries!"

Jaime rushed over to Lizzy, and threw her arms around her. Even Heidi jumped up in her lap, and licked her peppermint coated face. Squirrel looked for treats, as one would expect from a science mentor.

Shannon had to ask, "Lizzy, why the despair? We are right here."

"I don't know," Lizzy cried. "I just feel, we will never find those oysters."

Squirrel tugged on the Captain's pantaloon. He reached down, and picked her up, and she licked his cheek. This caused him to turn his head. He looked at Lizzy with his other eye fully opened. "Lieutenant, what be ye sittin' on?"

She answered, "Kind of a large, sad-looking purple rock. It's perfect for sitting. Looks like half an egg sticking out of the ground."

Jaime punched her arm, "Isn't that what we are looking for, Master Purveyor? A large, purple egg shaped rock, half buried?"

"Well I…hold it! Stop the presses! Lost expedition found! Master Purveyor discovers rare artifact! Lieutenant Lizzy saves party! Artifact found by superior brain! Crew eternally grateful!"

Shannon saved Squirrel the trouble, she wrote a note and handed it to the dackel: **Oh, brother!!!**

Jaime said, "If you notice, she's sitting on her superior brain."

There it was, the Glorp, right under Lizzy with just a slight hint of a frown etched into its features. The Olde Salte, and the other assortments moved the rock, and rolled it to the left. Underneath, were seven Rocky Mountain Oysters in a scientifically pristine habitat, all on the half shell. (Seven would just be enough for a pinochle tournament.)

"Well, Lieutenant Lizzy, I be takin' your camera, and documenting this historic occasion. You did bring your camera for just such a purpose?"

"Well, Captain. You see, it was on my list of supplies for CPO Jaime to carry, but it was number 542 on my list, and I guess Jaime forgot to bring it. I guess, that's why CPO's need officers."

Jaime started in on her. "Lizzy, that is the one item that the Captain expressly asked <u>you</u> to bring and…" She looked around. "Where are the doggies?"

Neither dachshund was in sight All of the others rushed to the scientifically, pristine habitat.

On the ground, in front of each dachshund were all the half shells belonging to the Rocky Mountain Oysters, and nothing else. Heidi had removed several ketchup packets from her eye patch reservoir, and all were opened. Apparently, 'our mentor, our teacher, our science conference speaker' brought the salt and pepper out from her attaché case.

Sheepishly, Squirrel nosed a note over to Shannon: **They were scientifically delicious.**

Lara's Place part deux

Seeing that they had eaten them all, and with no other Glorps in sight, the Captain started his charges onward up to Valley Top. No one noticed the slight smile etched onto the face of the Glorp.

The group finally made it the crest of Valley Top Mountain, and descended into the main attraction of the valley, Le Café Bowl-A-Far, otherwise known as Lara's Place. It is a totally transparent diner, completely built out of crystal glass, and in certain areas, frozen ice. (All attempts to use unfrozen ice proved structurally unsound.) Looking through the walls, they could tell that they were the last to arrive.

Sitting nearest the entrance were the yardapes, and the two smallest assortments quaffing root beer. Over on the other side were Carrie and Josslyn. It appeared, Carrie was distracting the waiter, and Josslyn was removing his 'see through' nametag. (Perhaps, they always wanted a nametag that said, 'Marvin'.) Up at the front, near the dais were Melissa Flower, Over-priced, Paiged, and Ema-San. They were sitting at the main table with the guest of honor, the suffering, Mr. Cracker.

Melissa reserved enough chairs for the Captain to sit with Mr. C, and then Shannon, Jaime, and finally Lizzy. Filling up the remaining seats of the diner were all, or most of the Pedelkees. (One never knows. Sometimes, the Pedelkees often count themselves twice.)

The Captain's entourage was welcomed in, and brought to the table. Mister Cracker stood, as did the Captain, while the ladies were seated. Before the Captain could sit, a passel of Pedelkees came, and brought him his navy blue sailing coat with white cap, and white leggings. The customary peg leg went unused. Enough Pedelkees came up and formed a changing area for him to dress, and he was seated in a jiffy. As for the dachshunds, seeing that they were not seated at the main table, Heidi and Squirrel joined the yardape table.

As all were finally seated, the hostess, owner, and executive chef of Café Bowl-A-Far came, and greeted the guests at the main table. Lara is a very tall, thin, brunette lady wearing an all-white ensemble with matching white cap. She carries a hint of aftershave, and has just the slightest French accent. "Bonjour! Moi ess Madame Lara. Welcome to mon place. Eet ess an honaire to have vou as mon guests. I zee zat all have now arrived at zee tables." Both gentlemen stood, and warmly shook her hand. "Eet ess my pleasaire to have all of vou as mon guests. Before dineeng, we weel have some entertainment by Monsieur…Wait! What ess zat horrible racket?"

All eyes turned toward the left side of the room. Sir Harold was demonstrating his ability to play Heidi as a flute-a-phone. He was blowing on her tummy, and   she was howling.

The others were blowing root beer out of their noses. Immediately, Lara rushed over to their table. "Leetle man, put down zee doggie. Do not show me zee badge, vou have no authority ici. Moi am zee law. Leetle dog, do not roll zee eyes at moi. Moi zees everytheeng. Un more outburst from any of vou, even vou, Mademoiselle Petaireson, and out zee beeldeeng, vou goes. All of vou. Remember, een Lara's Place, zee doggie bag ess not just le expression. Capeesh? Everyone shook their heads, affirmatively.

"As moi was saying, zere ess entertainment, Monsieur Over-Priced."

The officially, approved goat racer could sing! His version of *Sailing*, brought the ole Captain to tears. Paiged accompanied him by placing ships into bottles over her head with her feet. These were sold to raise money for riding camp.

As Over-Priced finished, Ms. Lara came up and thanked him. Then she said, "Moi hopes zat vou are hungree. We are starting with zee appetizer, cold vichyssoise. Like revenge, eet ess best served cold. Eenjoy!"

This was the moment that Squirrel was waiting for. Heidi and she were best friends, but there was the little matter of a vacuum sweeper in their past. Dachshunds and especially dackels, strive not to get even, but hopefully, get one ahead. Standing between Heidi and Squirrel was a floor lamp with large lamp shade that extended over both of them. While Heidi was enjoying her vichyssoise, Ms. Peterson pulled a very small container from her attaché case, and opened the pop-up lid. Very slowly, a small, brown, June bug crawled from the can. Without anyone noticing, Squirrel flipped the bug right over Heidi's head, and it landed on the lampshade.

It began to buzz. Heidi's ears perked up, and seeing the June bug, she leaped for it. She crashed into the lampshade, tearing through in two places. Heidi had missed the bug, which had the foresight to escape the building, but she was trapped on the lamp support. Struggling to free herself, she crashed the lamp onto her table, and managed to tiddlywink a bowl of soup onto Jason's head. Cold vichyssoise seeped down his body. It was the closest, he came to a bath all week. Needless to say, this got everyone's attention. Sarah and Rachel came to Jason's rescue, and using napkins, cleaned him up the best they could. It would have gone quicker, but they were laughing too hard. Harold was spooning the soup off of Jason, and eating it. Nothing goes to waste in a yardape's world.

Jason could only mutter, "I have been vichyssoise-d by my own pertack docksoon!"

Mr. Cracker, the Olde Salte of a Sailor, and Shannon Bo-Bannon rushed over to help, but it seemed all under control. Everyone looked at Heidi. She was mortified! She turned her entire body, so she could not look at anyone. Shannon said, "Aw, Squirrel's comforting her." Squirrel <u>was</u> licking Heidi, but really was just enjoying the soup.

It was then, that Ms. Lara arrived at the table. "What have zee doggees done to mon table? Ma Lampe! Ma Soupe! Bad doggees! (Heidi cringed even more.) Why cannot zee sheepsdog behave like zee **noted** dachshund?" She snapped her fingers, and help arrived to finish cleaning up the mess. Part of her cleanup crew was Marvin, and he was missing a nametag.

Ms. Lara continued, "We have fine food, fine entertainment, and fine company, and zees ess how moi am repaid? Everyboody out! Moi diner ess closed! Teel furthaire noteese."

"But Ms. Lara," argued the Captain, "we will pay all damages."

"Of course, vou weel! And zee suffereeng Monsieur Cracker will take hees geeft with heem. Come here, soups boy!" She motioned to Jason. "Take zee box, and give it to heem!" It was a box with air holes.

"Open it, boy. Show me what's in it," requested Mr. Cracker.

Jason opened the box, and out popped a gold, gray and black, striped, tabby cat. It was wearing a black beret with a candy cigarette in its mouth. On its collar was a card that said, its name was *Jacque Dahmeet*. The dachshunds were not amused at the new arrival. They recognized competition or much worse.

Jaime pulled on Mr. Cracker's vest and asked, "In English, doesn't Jacque Dahmeet mean, Jack Da...?"

He stopped her, "Hush child, this is a family show!"

The Pedelkee Steamer   an SW Production

www.ingramcontent.com/pod-product-compliance
Lightning Source LLC
Chambersburg PA
CBHW081230020426
42331CB00012B/3117